To Rosamund & Frank.
with love,
from Betty and Nicholas.
1996

The Illawarra

BETWEEN THE MOUNTAINS AND THE SEA

Photography by SUE and BRIAN KENDRICK

Text by GILLIAN CUMMING

A Lightstorm Publication

Published by Lightstorm Publishing ©
Designed by Lightstorm Graphics
Distributed by Lightstorm Photography
P.O. Box 1167 Nowra NSW 2541
Ph: (044) 466 007 Fax: (044) 466 008

Hanimex Pty Ltd
108 Old Pittwater Road
Brookvale NSW 2100
Ph: (02) 9938 0400

All the photographs in this book were taken on Fuji transparency film. For landscape work, Fuji Velvia was chosen for its rich colours and excellent sharpness. Fuji Provia 100, with its faithful colour rendition and beautiful contrast, was the film of choice for aerial and portraiture photography while Provia 400 was chosen in low light situations where a high film speed was required. For action and sports photography Fuji's extraordinary Super G Plus 800 film was chosen, not only for its high speed and remarkable fineness of grain but its tolerance under difficult lighting conditions.

Title Page: Wollongong lights up! The unforgettable sight of Wollongong at twilight, viewed from the Panorama Hotel Restaurant atop Bulli Pass. The industrial area for which the region is best known can be seen in the distance, as can the ships anchored offshore, awaiting entry to Port Kembla Harbour.

Right: An aerial view of Wollongong Harbour, with the industrial heartland of Port Kembla visible in the background.

Overleaf (clockwise from top left): Children from the Australian Turkish Association perform a traditional Turkish dance for fans at the Steelers Stadium; Minnamurra Falls, Budderoo National Park; Flowers of the Illawarra Flame Tree, Brachychiton acerfolius; Surf-lifesaver at North Wollongong Beach; Kiama's famous painted cow, outside the Old Fire Station Community Arts Centre; Loading the Iron Whyalla at the Port Kembla Coal Terminal; Cycling brothers Tim, Joshua and Ben Kersten, riding towards the Sydney 2000 Olympics; Coal miners of the Illawarra at the end of shift.

C O N T E N T S

INTRODUCTION

There is nothing more breathtaking than the view of the Illawarra from Bulli Pass, high on top of the escarpment. Viewed again from Stanwell Tops, the Illawarra meanders south into the distance – beaches fringed by a blanket of blue, rocky outcrops, industry then city and suburbia edging great tracts of rural greenery that climb into the dense growth of the towering escarpment. For locals, it is panoramas such as these that offer great comfort when returning home from a long journey. For visitors, these are images never to be forgotten.

The name Illawarra is derived from the language of the local Aboriginal people, who came from north of Australia sometime between 20,000 and 40,000 years ago. Although it has had a mixture of meanings over the years, it is generally regarded as describing a pleasant place near the sea.

Beginning less than an hour's drive south of Sydney, the Illawarra's 1128 square kilometres comprise the local government areas of Wollongong, Shellharbour and Kiama. Home to more than 250,000 people, the region snakes along 85 kilometres of the New South Wales coastline from the Royal National Park in the north to Kiama in the south. To the west, the Illawarra is flanked by the magnificent escarpment that becomes the Southern Tableland, while beyond to the south lies the Shoalhaven district.

Lake Illawarra is an impressive focal point for the region. Bounded by Wollongong in the north and Shellharbour in the south, the natural saltwater lagoon is a haven for fish and birdlife and is also popular for fishing and watersports.

Explorers George Bass and Matthew Flinders became the first Europeans to visit the region when they accidentally landed the *Tom Thumb* at Towradgi Beach in 1796. The Illawarra's coal potential was discovered by accident soon afterwards, but difficulties with access to the region meant it was timber and not black coal that finally led Europeans to settle here. Pastoralists followed in 1815 when Liverpool farmer Dr Charles Throsby hacked a route across the Southern Tableland in search of feed for his drought-stricken

Left: The Illawarra's popular beachfront cycleway stretches for more than 40 kms. from Thirroul to Shellharbour. Enjoyed by cyclists, roller bladers, walkers and joggers, the cycleway offers magnificent views of the region's golden beaches and towering escarpment.

Right: Map courtesy of J.K. Craigie ©

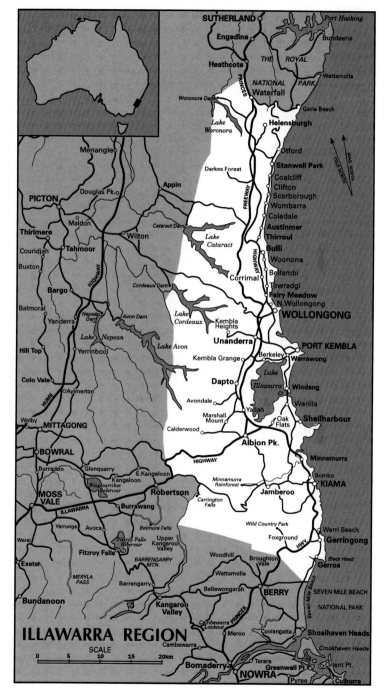

ILLAWARRA REGION

cattle. Grazing, cropping and dairying thrived and the Illawarra became known as the 'Garden of New South Wales'.

By the mid-1800s, the problems associated with mining the region's rich coal reserves had been overcome and collieries were developed in the region's north and north-west, boosting the development of business and government infrastructure around the thriving settlement of Wollongong. Industrial development followed early this century when Charles Hoskins' iron and steel works commenced production in 1931. Hoskins' dream led to the creation of BHP, known internationally as 'the Big Australian'. From one century to the next, the Illawarra shifted from a busy farming community towards development of mining and industry. Today this might remains centred on Wollongong's industrial heartland, Port Kembla.

The people of the Illawarra come from more than 80 countries, making this region the most ethnically diverse non-metropolitan area in Australia. The region's beauty has always captured the imaginations of artists and writers, from Eugene von Guérard's pastoral plains and lush rainforests painted in the mid-1800s to contemporary talents such as sculptor Bert Flugelman and writer Peter Corris. The Illawarra also nurtured the talents of aviation pioneer Lawrence Hargrave, who late last century carried out his box-kite experiments on Stanwell Park Beach.

The region's wide-ranging educational facilities are led by the University of Wollongong, which is ranked among the top nine universities nationally, and Illawarra sportspeople continue to be world leaders in a range of endeavours, from motorcycle racing to cycling and surfing.

Whereas Wollongong has developed into the industrial and commercial powerhouse of the region, Shellharbour is now a thriving residential and water recreational area while seaside Kiama with its famous blowhole, is regarded as a tourist mecca.

Recreationally, the Illawarra has something for everyone – fishing, surfing, sailing, bushwalking, hanggliding and cycling. As a result, tourism is now a powerful economic force in the region as people discover the Illawarra's diverse, natural beauty.

The Illawarra - best kept secret in New South Wales!

Left: The air still heavy with water vapour of a recent shower, a couple enjoy the 1.6 km. loop boardwalk through the Minnamurra Rainforest. While the coastal plain receives an annual rainfall of about 1200mm. the highest parts of the escarpment receive as much as 1800mm. each year.

H I S T O R Y

ABORIGINAL HISTORY

Some time during the last Ice Age, between 20,000 and 40,000 years ago, when Borneo, Java and South-East Asia were linked, dark-skinned people made their way to the Australian continent. Traditionally hunters and gatherers, these indigenous people moved in small tribes to where food was plentiful. Before long, the coastal Illawarra's fertile soil, lush vegetation and abundance of food was supporting growing numbers of Aborigines. The obstacle of the Great Divide is thought to have prevented Illawarra Aborigines moving to higher lands, where food was harder to find and where indigenous populations were smaller.

By the time Europeans set foot in the Illawarra there were five coastal Aboriginal tribes. Nomadic and semi-nomadic, from north to south they were known as the Dharawal, Wadi Wadi, Gurandad, Dharumba and Wandandian people. They moved to where native foods were seasonal or where religious, social or ceremonial needs dictated. Sometimes this meant travelling long distances and the trails created were later used by Europeans and even became roads.

The names Illawarra and Wollongong, along with many other place names used today, are derived from the oral languages of the region's Aboriginal population. The word Illawarra is meant to convey 'a pleasant place' or 'a high and pleasant place near the sea', while Wollongong is thought to mean hard or high ground near water. It has also been explained as the sound of waves breaking on sand and as a derivative of the name of an early Aborigine, Woolonglow, whose descendants still live locally.

Aborigines were bound by kinship and religion. Marriage occurred with someone from outside a clan and men could have more than one wife. While men were responsible for social, political and religious customs, women cared for their immediate family and provided most of the food needs. Men

Left: This detail from the stunning tile mural on the foreshore at Shellharbour was designed and executed by the Coomaditchi Artists' Co-operative with input from tile muralists Tori de Mestre and Cynthia Turner and Aboriginal children from the area.

hunted with spears hafted with chips of quartz and fished using multi-pronged bone-tipped spears. They often fished the coast at night with torches fashioned from beaten and tied bark and would drag bream from shallows with their hands. Women fished with shell hook and line and gathered vegetable matter, shellfish, small mammals and reptiles.

Nature provided not only the food needs of the indigenous population, but all their requirements for living. Bark was cut from trees to make canoes and overhanging rocks provided shelter, which Aborigines marked with drawings or paintings in charcoal and ochre. Tools included boomerangs, spears and digging sticks as well as fishing lines, hooks and multi-pronged fishing spears made from stone, shell, bone, hair and plant material. In winter, possum skins were worn to keep warm while for decoration head bands of kangaroo teeth were worn and bones were pushed through men's noses. The temperate climate and abundant food supply of the region are thought to have offered the Illawarra's indigenous population a good lifestyle.

Middens of the shell remains of Aboriginal tribes' basic diet can be found around Lake Illawarra, Bass Point and other locations across the region. Excavation of these middens, as well as the uncovering of campsites and the discovery of shelters adorned with engravings, drawings and paintings, has revealed valuable information about the diet and lifestyle of the area's original inhabitants. Illawarra engravings have been found to represent humans, birds, fish and mythological figures.

Following European contact and settlement, traditional tribal life was progressively eroded as the indigenous people's social and economic systems fell apart and introduced diseases such as small pox, influenza, measles and syphilis took their toll. It is estimated that there were about 3000 full-blood Aborigines in the Illawarra in 1820, but by the turn of the century only a handful remained. Descendants of these traditional tribal Aborigines, people who prize their heritage and maintain certain traditions, live in the Illawarra today.

EXPLORATION AND SETTLEMENT

The first sighting of the Illawarra by Europeans is thought to have occurred from afar in 1770 when Captain James Cook was heading north to where his eventual landing of the *Endeavour* took place at Botany Bay. On his voyage Cook almost set foot on land near Woonona, today a suburb north of Wollongong, but his landing party was defeated by rough sea. The party did, however observe a small number of dark-skinned people on the shore edge and Cook noted in his log a landmark he named Red Point, thought to be Port Kembla. He also described as 'the crown of a hat' a landmark believed to be Mount Kembla.

Many ships sailed past over the ensuing years, but the Illawarra remained largely unexplored by Europeans, mainly due to the region's lack of a natural harbour. Also, the mountain range to the west formed a natural barrier, too difficult for settlers to penetrate. It wasn't until a quarter of a century after Cook's sail past that explorers George Bass and Matthew Flinders accidentally landed in the region in 1796. While searching for Port Hacking, their small boat *Tom Thumb* was blown further south and eventually washed ashore somewhere near Towradgi, south of Cook's attempted Woonona landing. Afterwards, Bass and Flinders entered Lake Illawarra, naming it Tom Thumb Lagoon, although a lagoon north of Port Kembla was given that name erroneously some time later.

The following year the region received some unexpected visitors– survivors of the shipwrecked *Sydney Cove*. From a party of 17 that set out from near Cape Everard in Victoria, bound for Sydney Town, only three members were eventually rescued by Sydney fishermen who noticed the smoke of a coal fire near Coalcliff. Later that year George Bass returned to investigate the region's coal potential. He reported observing several seams of coal in the towering cliffs buttressing the ocean, but the difficulty of transporting coal from an isolated region to Sydney proved too great and the Illawarra remained largely undisturbed.

Eight years later, in 1805, it was timber and not black coal that ultimately led to the region's settlement and development when

Left: The first recorded visit by Europeans to the Illawarra occurred when explorers Bass and Flinders accidentally landed near Towradgi in 1796 while searching for Port Hacking. This re-enactment, by members of Theatre South, commemorated the bicentenary of Bass and Flinders' historic voyage in the 'Tom Thumb'.

Right: The Breakwater Light at Wollongong Harbour is one of only two cast iron and boiler plate lighthouses in Australia. Erected in 1871, the 13m-high lighthouse originally had an acetylene gas lamp before changing to electric light in 1916.

Government surveyor James Meehan reported that dense cedar forests stood in the Illawarra. Still, it wasn't until 1812 that cedar cutters began to arrive, cutting large trees into planks that were carried or pulled to the top of Bulli where they were hauled by bullock to Parramatta then on to Sydney. Later, cedar was hauled to the beach and onto boats bound for Sydney.

By 1815, graziers had begun driving cattle into the Illawarra. Leading the way was Liverpool farmer Dr Charles Throsby, who hacked a route across the tableland in search of feed for his drought-stricken cattle. Looking down on the Illawarra from the escarpment, he was not disappointed by the green vista before him. The following year Governor Lachlan Macquarie directed that Crown land be reserved and land grants be established.

As red cedar continued to be taken from the region, settlers moved in and established farms on cleared land. By 1826, the settlement close to where boats anchored on the coast became known as Wollongong. Three years later soldiers were stationed there to control illegal cedar cutting, warn off bushrangers and escaped convicts, prevent degradation of the indigenous population and protect settlers.

Local Government began operation in 1843 when Governor Gipps established the Illawarra District Council, which had responsibilities as far south as the Shoalhaven River. That same year, the introduction of clearing leases enabled pioneer Caroline Chisholm to settle immigrants on fertile land in Shellharbour. Grazing was eventually overtaken by cropping and dairying, which produced grain, vegetables and butter for the Sydney market. The following year the opening of Bulli Pass improved road access between Sydney and the Illawarra and created a breathtaking entry to the region.

By the mid-1800s, the supply of cedar was almost exhausted and agriculture was becoming of secondary importance to the development of the region's greatest natural asset – high-grade

Left: Large spreading fig trees and stonewall pastures characterise the dairy farming country in the south of the region.

Above right: Known as 'red gold' by the timber cutters who worked the region from 1812, red cedar was once abundant in the rainforest of the Illawarra. Growing straight and tall, the fragrant and durable timber was put to many uses by the growing colony, from fence posts to flooring and furniture. Although red cedar trees are not uncommon in the region today, the rainforest giants of yesteryear are rare.

Right: The Pilot's Cottage on Blowhole Point at Kiama was built in 1880 to house the officer in charge of the port and his family. These days the beautifully restored building, which features basalt walls, cedar joinery and iron bark flooring, houses an historical museum.

black coal. Spurred by the success of James Schoobert, who in 1849 succeeded in opening the region's first coal mine at Mt Keira, Wollongong shifted from being a busy farming community towards becoming the industrial giant it is today. By 1880, 10 coal pits were open around Wollongong and mining villages had begun to mushroom northwards. But despite the advent of coal, in the outlying areas of Shellharbour and Kiama dairying continued to flourish and in the 1880s the region was highly regarded as the 'Garden of New South Wales'.

The completion of the Illawarra rail line in 1888 proved crucial to the region's trade and progress. Locals and visitors were no longer dependent on ship transport in and out of the area or on having to negotiate the terrible roads and mountainous approaches by coach and cart. Overnight, access to the Illawarra had became relatively easy and visitors from Sydney soon discovered the pleasures of the region's scenic beauty. The upgrading of Wollongong Harbour in 1895 and the creation, more than 30 years later, of a large deep-water harbour at Port Kembla served to support the region's burgeoning industrial base.

By the early 1930s Charles Hoskins' iron and steel works had commenced production of steel on land west of Port Kembla, and in 1935 the company was sold to the Broken Hill Propriety Company (BHP). An ambitious program of expansion followed and today, BHP's multi-million dollar Illawarra operations employ more than 12,000 people.

These days the Illawarra is recognised around the world for its progressive industrial base. Modern transport means that the region is within an hour's drive of Sydney. Both locals and visitors enjoy an area of stunning beauty and a lifestyle that combines the best of contemporary urban living and rural getaways.

Left: Built in 1939 in the Elizabethan Revival style, historic Gleniffer Brae was the family home of Sidney Hoskins, father of steel-making in the Illawarra. Designed by architect Geoffrey Loveridge, the Keiraville manor house later served as a private girls' school but is now home to the Conservatorium of Music.

Above right: This evocative bronze statue honouring the region's coal mining heritage was created by local sculptor Liz Johnson. Depicting a contemporary miner with his brother of yesteryear, the monument was erected in 1995 outside Wollongong Council Offices.

Right: Nestled into the hillside at Jamberoo, St Matthews Catholic Church is one of four delightful stone churches in the town built in the latter half of last century.

NATURAL ENVIRONMENT

Black coal might be the Illawarra's most valuable natural asset but, economics aside, residents and visitors to the Illawarra are more likely to favour the region's emerald green forests, lush parks and gardens and countless golden beaches and waterways.

The Illawarra is straddled by green corridors and laced by national parks, state forests and tracts of privately held escarpment land. Eastwards, the region's lowland kisses the Pacific Ocean at beaches and rocky outcrops that curve along more than 85 kilometres of coastline. To the south, Lake Illawarra is a haven for watersports and, bordering Kiama, the Minnamurra River is an important water habitat and fish nursery, also popular with anglers.

THE AQUATIC ENVIRONMENT

Bound by Wollongong in the north and Shellharbour on its southern shores, Lake Illawarra is the largest body of water in the region. Like most of NSW's coastal saltwater lagoons, it is broad and shallow, measuring 9.5 kilometres long and 5.5 kilometres wide. In its deepest parts it measures 3.7 metres, though there are extensive areas of shallower water. The lake is a haven for fish and birdlife, but also offers a myriad of water-based recreational activities, including prawning, fishing, sailing, sailboarding, water skiing, canoeing and paddleboating. In recent years, initiatives by the Lake Illawarra Authority have been instrumental in improving the water quality of the lake and transforming its foreshores into an attractive recreational area.

Numerous small creeks and waterways across the region snake their way from high within the escarpment down to the ocean foreshores. In Kiama, the Minnamurra River is the largest river in the region. Its mangrove-lined banks and natural vegetation are an important breeding place for water birds and its watery depths make an ideal fish nursery. The river's freshwater reaches, along

Previous pages: The Kingsford Smith Memorial Lookout at Gerroa overlooks the sweeping expanse of Seven Mile Beach. In 1933 'Smithy' used a long, smooth section of the beach to commence his second crossing of the Tasman aboard his plane the 'Southern Cross'.
Left: In the far north of the region the escarpment meets the sea in dramatic cliffs of Hawkesbury sandstone.
Right: Cathedral Rocks is situated 3kms north of Kiama, at the southern end of Jones Beach. This distinctive volcanic rock, formed more than 250 million years ago, has lured visitors since 1890.

with streams such as Mullet Creek and Macquarie Rivulet, are rare wetlands. Killalea wetland in Shellharbour is probably the least disturbed freshwater wetland in the region, while small coastal lagoons such as Spring Creek at Bombo and Werri Lagoon at Gerroa provide important habitat for water birds and are popular picnic spots. Tom Thumb Lagoon, adjacent to Australia's Industry World, is undergoing a community–run regeneration program that has already seen native flora and fauna return to the wetland.

Illawarra's lakes, rivers and waterways support a vast range of birdlife, including more than 20 species of migratory bird, some rare. Waterfowls, swans and pelicans are commonly seen across the region, along with grey teal, grebes, black cormorants, egrets, ibis, spoonbills, herons, sea eagles, stilt, curlews and reed warblers.

Westwards, the mountains meet blue water at favourite picnic sites Cordeaux, Cataract and Avon dams. These dams, now stunning lakes surrounded by forest, are perched high above the coast in the region's north. Avon Dam supplies water to customers from Scarborough to Gerroa whilst Cordeaux and Cataract Dams are dedicated as back-up supplies for the Illawarra and the Sydney metropolitan area.

Sheltered rock pools and swimming holes, as well as seaside saltwater pools, are popular with young and old, be they swimmers, surfers, snorkellers or scuba divers. Bushrangers Bay Aquatic Reserve at Bass Point, south of Shellharbour township, was dedicated as an aquatic reserve in 1983 to protect the diversity of underwater habitats in its sheltered waters. Favoured by snorkellers and scuba divers, the pristine bay's shallow waters harbour more than 35 species of fish as well as oysters, shellfish and other marine life.

Surfing hot spots include 'The Farm', Mystics Beach, South Shellharbour Beach and Killalea Beach, while for swimmers, patrolled beaches dot the coastline from Stanwell Park in the north to Bombo Beach in the south.

Right: Lake Illawarra, located between Wollongong and Shellharbour, is a focus for water-based recreational activities in the region. Initiatives by the Lake Illawarra Authority in recent years have been instrumental in transforming the lake's waters and foreshores into an attractive recreational area. Algae has been cleared to improve water quality and boating access; wetlands have been constructed at Kully Bay, Warrawong, and Budjong Creek, Berkeley, to reduce the amount of nutrients and sediments that enter the lake; and jetties, boat launching facilities and recreational facilities have been developed on the foreshore.

LANDSCAPE OF THE ILLAWARRA

The Illawarra is bordered by the Royal National Park in the north and Seven Mile Beach National Park in the south. Inbetween, the region is dotted with numerous parks and gardens.

The escarpment, a stunning backdrop to the entire region, rises abruptly from the Pacific Ocean, climbing to more than 300 metres in the north and over twice this elevation west of Kiama. The most dominant feature of the Illawarra landscape, the escarpment is used by bushwalkers, rock climbers, abseilers, paragliders and hanggliders. Lookouts at Stanwell Tops, Sublime Point, Mount Keira and Mount Kembla provide stunning panoramas of the Illawarra.

Nestled into the side of the escarpment at leafy Mount Pleasant in Wollongong is the magnificent Rhododendron Park, where thousands of varieties of rhododendrons and azaleas thrive in cool, moist, conditions to create mass colour shows throughout spring. Popular with picnickers and a regular venue for weddings, the park is cared for by members of the Australian Rhododendron Society.

Wollongong's green corridor includes the beautiful Botanic Garden edging the escarpment at Keiraville, plus its annexes Mt Keira Summit Park, Korrungulla Wetlands near Windang, Kelly's Falls at Stanwell Tops and Puckey's Estate on the foreshore at North Wollongong. The 20-hectare Puckey's Estate is one of only two remnant hind dune lagoon complexes between Port Hacking and Lake Illawarra. Its diverse vegetation and close proximity to Wollongong's CBD makes Puckey's an area of significance to be preserved.

The Botanic Garden at Keiraville is host to plants from dry and wet tropical areas and temperate climates. A favourite destination for visitors and wedding parties is the sunken rose garden where 2000 rose shrubs bloom annually. There's also an azalea bank, a rainforest and a woodland garden displaying perennials, camelias and magnolias aplenty. Close by a miniature lake dotted

Left: Wollongong's special relationship with sister city Kawasaki was commemorated in 1993 with this gift – a 10 m-long traditional Japanese bridge built by Kawasaki craftsmen in the grounds of the Wollongong Botanic Garden.

Above right: Rhododendron Park is home to the largest planting of Vireya tropical rhododendrons in Australia, such as the superb Vireya macgregorai pictured here. It also boasts an impressive planting of tall and rare trees, magnolias and camelias.

Right: A mature example of the strangler fig, Ficus destruens, which begins life in a branch or fork of a host tree. Its roots descend to the ground, thickening and spreading until they enclose and strangle the host tree, leading to its eventual death.

with waterlillies, a traditional Japanese bridge crosses to an avenue of powder pink cherry blossoms, overlooked by a traditional Japanese teahouse – both gifts to Wollongong from its sister city Kawasaki in Japan.

Shellharbour's Macquarie Pass National Park covers 1000 hectares, 10 kilometres west of suburban Albion Park. Fed by Macquarie Rivulet, the park harbours magnificent sub-tropical rainforest and superb waterfalls. There are numerous walking tracks, several natural swimming pools and three picnic areas, including Clover Hill overlooking Macquarie Falls.

Also located within Shellharbour is the 250-hectare Blackbutt Reserve, the Illawarra's last remaining tract of coastal plain forest. The reserve is a popular venue for walking and get-togethers and has barbecue facilities, a playground and an open-air amphitheatre.

The Killalea State Recreation Area curves along the coastline from Bass Point to Kiama. Aboriginal middens as well as one of the Illawarra's few littoral rainforest areas lie within this important reserve.

Minnamurra Rainforest, Australia's southernmost sub-tropical rainforest, is only a 10-minute drive from Jamberoo. Established in 1986 as part of the Budderoo National Park, the award-winning microcosm has been made more accessible via a 1.6 kilometre loop boardwalk that enables viewing of the rainforest for young, old and disabled. A sanctuary for native lyrebirds, which are commonly seen and heard, Minnamurra also supports populations of honeyeaters, King parrots, kookaburras and yellow-throated scrub wrens. Reptiles include the red-bellied black snake and diamond python and there are colonies of platypus, eels and crayfish. This rare tract of sub-tropical rainforest is also a habitat for more than 120 vegetative species of plant life, including the sand-paper fig, native hibiscus, white cedar, stag horns and unusual looking fungi of various shapes and colour. Two-thirds of all fern species found in New South Wales are found at Minnamurra and red cedars that survived the early timber cutters are among the biggest trees.

Left: Located within Budderoo National Park the spectacular Minnamurra Falls can be viewed while on a 4.2 km loop walk. After following the Minnamurra Rainforest boardwalk, a steep climb leads to a viewing platform where the 42 m-high lower falls and the 20 m-high upper falls (pictured here) can be observed.

Right: Giant tree ferns, Cynthea antartica, thrive in the rainforest of the escarpment, where their slender trunks support fronds that spread to more than two metres.

A REGIONAL VIEW

One of the Illawarra's greatest assets is its geographic diversity. Backdropped by the magnificent escarpment, there are few places in the Illawarra that do not afford breathtaking vistas of emerald green hillsides, inland waters or ocean beaches. Whereas Wollongong is the economic and industrial heartland of the region, it shares with Shellharbour and Kiama inviting pockets of country quiet, popular with residents and visitors alike.

WOLLONGONG REGION

It was cedar, not coal, that attracted Europeans to the Illawarra in 1812 and eventually led to Wollongong's settlement. After dense cedar forests were felled for the Sydney timber market, graziers and settlers moved in to establish farms on cleared land. By 1826, the coastal settlement known as Wollongong was producing meat, vegetable and dairy products for local and Sydney markets.

Although black coal was first sighted in the ocean cliffs of the north during the closing years of the 19th century, the region's inaccessibility and the difficulty of transporting heavy raw materials to Sydney delayed mining. As a result, Wollongong remained a pioneering farming community until the mid-1800s when coal mining at last became viable and mining villages began to mushroom northwards. As industry developed, these villages merged and Wollongong grew to become one of Australia's biggest industrial cities.

Previous pages: Mt Keira Lookout offers a stunning panoramic view over the city of Wollongong. Walking trails, a hangglider launching platform, a restaurant and barbecue facilities are available for visitors to the lookout.

Left: A place of beauty and history, Wollongong Harbour's stone walls offer protection to both pleasure craft and the town's commercial fishing fleet. Above Wollongong Harbour at Flagstaff Point is Wollongong Lighthouse, erected in 1937 to warn passing ships of the dangers of Bellambi Reef to the north and the Five Islands to the south.

Above right: The escarpment peaks of Mt Keira and Mt Kembla dominate the Wollongong skyline. Mt Kembla was first described by Europeans in 1770 when Captain Cook noted in his log a landmark that resembled the 'crown of a hat'. Both mountains offer stunning views of the city.

Right: A top spot for holidaymakers and locals, North Wollongong Beach is patrolled by a willing team of surf lifesavers seven days a week from October until Easter.

Instrumental to this growth was the completion of the Illawarra rail line in 1888 and, early in the new century, the construction of a deep-sea port at Port Kembla. Perhaps more important for Wollongong, however, was the influence of industrialist Charles Hoskins, whose 1920s purchase of 162 hectares of land west of Port Kembla and vision for the future was a deciding factor in shaping Illawarra industry. Hoskins' iron and steel works eventually became Australian Iron and Steel, which in 1935 was sold to Broken Hill Proprietary Company Limited (BHP).

Before long, Wollongong built a reputation as a steel city, an image it proudly displays today as it shifts towards new technology and the ever-expanding international market.

The City of Wollongong stretches for more than 60 kilometres along the coastline, from Helensburgh in the north to Windang and Dapto in the south and south-west. Ranked as NSW's third largest city, after Sydney and Newcastle, Wollongong is by far the Illawarra's largest population centre with 182,000 people. Even though Wollongong covers an area of 715 square kilometres, the heavy industry for which the city is mainly known is concentrated in the industrial heartland of Port Kembla, several kilometres south of the city. Built on reclaimed swampland, the gigantic industrial centre has its own deep-water port and is fed by a string of collieries that mine the escarpment and mountain plateau to the north.

While Wollongong has all the amenities of contemporary, urban living, its lineal coastal development means that it has retained easy access to beaches and parks, forests and mountain.

Above left: With reliable on-shore winds and steep drop-offs for launching, hanggliding has become a favourite recreation at Stanwell Tops. Here, a thrill-seeker comes into land after an exciting ride with one of the experienced operators who offer tandem flights from Bald Hill.

Left: Coal miners' cottages were built in the region's northern suburbs once the industry started to boom in the mid-1800s. The tiny dwellings, such as these renovated cottages at Coledale, were home to the miner, his wife and perhaps 10 children.

Right: Surfing is a popular pastime throughout the region but it is only at Wollongong Beach that one sees scenes such as this—crystal blue water, perfect waves and surfers backdropped by the industrial heartland of Port Kembla.

SHELLHARBOUR REGION

Although explorers, graziers and cedar cutters visited Shellharbour from as early as 1796, it wasn't until the 1830s that Europeans began to settle the area. Cattle grazing dates back to 1803 and cedar cutters worked the district without permission from 1810, but when rural pioneer and philanthropist Caroline Chisholm brought 23 families to the Shellharbour area in 1843 the population almost doubled overnight.

By then, timber cutting licences had been introduced and new settlers were able to obtain clearing leases, which consisted of about 50 hectares of natural bush. Each family was given seven, rent-free years to clear the land and establish a self-sufficient farm. Chisholm eventually settled immigrants on about 1600 hectares around Shellharbour.

During the 19th century, cedar, lime, wheat, cattle, coal (at Tongarra) and basalt were eventually overshadowed by the area's thriving dairying industry. The name Shellharbour was in popular usage early in the area's settlement and aptly described the shell remains of Aboriginal middens found around the settlement's shores.

Today Shellharbour covers 154 square kilometres and its burgeoning population will soon tip 50,000. Declared a city in 1995, Shellharbour stretches from the southern side of Lake Illawarra and Macquarie Rivulet in the north to Macquarie Falls in the west and the Minnamurra River bordering Kiama in the south.

No longer a centre for dairying, Shellharbour is now a powerhouse for Illawarra residential development. Highly regarded as a mecca for water sports, Shellharbour has a protected boat harbour and Bass Point south of the township is popular for snorkelling and scuba diving. Lake Illawarra in the north is the perfect place for fishing, sailing, sailboarding, water skiing, canoeing and paddle boating. Prawning is popular through the summer months, when the lake becomes a fairyland of lights at night.

Left: Stretching into the distance south of the sand-barred entrance to Lake Illawarra is the City of Shellharbour. Bound by the lake in the north, the Pacific Ocean to the east and Minnamurra River to the south, Shellharbour is a mecca for watersports.

Above right: A detail from the striking wall mural at the amphitheatre in Blackbutt Reserve, painted by the Coomaditchi Artists' Co-operative and young Aboriginals from the area. Principal artist Lorraine Brown used dot technique and stylised imagery to depict animals from the area, such as the wallaby in this picture.

Right: Shellharbour's Bass Point is popular for beachside picnics, fishing, snorkelling and scuba diving. Many of the region's novice divers take their first plunge in the clear blue waters of Bass Point's Bushrangers Bay Aquatic Reserve.

KIAMA REGION

While explorer George Bass is credited for making the first recorded reference to Kiama in 1797, the seaside village's first European settler was cedar cutter David Smith. Cedar dominated the economy in the early years, but once its supply was exhausted dairying started to thrive. Keen to produce the best, through careful culling Kiama's pioneering dairymen developed the high milk yielding and hardy Illawarra Shorthorn breed of cattle from Ayrshire, Shorthorn and Devon stock. Australia's first cooperative butter factory was formed in the district and by 1869 had begun to export product overseas.

In the 1870s, basalt quarries began operation, eventually surpassing dairying in economic importance. Basalt (commonly called blue metal), used for road and rail base and concrete manufacture, continues to be quarried at Shellharbour and Kiama.

There is mixed opinion on the meaning of the name Kiama, with some historians believing it is derived from the Aboriginal Kiarama, thought to mean 'where the sea makes a noise'. Others say Kiama comes from the words Kiara Mia, meaning 'fertile district'. The first view associates the town's name to the Kiama Blowhole, one of the most distinct and popular attractions on the South Coast.

Bordered seawards by Norfolk Island pines, today Kiama is both a popular tourist destination and a desirable place to live for people working in the region. Situated only 30 minutes from the heart of Wollongong, the municipality covers 259 square kilometres from the Minnamurra River in the north to the Foxground boundary and the top of Jamberoo Pass in the west. Home to almost 18,000 people, the area includes the coastal villages of Gerringong and Gerroa to the south and the quaint village of Jamberoo nestled at the foot of the escarpment to the west.

Left: Kiama's famous blowhole was first reported by explorer George Bass, who thought it was the result of a volcanic eruption. In fact, the blowhole was formed by the action of air in a sea-worn cave. Compressed by waves, air in the cave forces a vertical passage upwards, eventually breaking through any incoming wave, which is forced upwards to 'blow'.

Above Right: Proud winner of the National Tidy Town title in 1995, the seaside village of Kiama comes alive each weekend when visitors are attracted to its markets and shops, jam packed with arts and crafts. The Terrace shops, which once housed workers of the town's basalt mine are the only example of timber terrace houses remaining in New South Wales.

Right: Completed in 1876, Kiama Harbour once catered to the area's growing shipping trade. These days it is used by pleasure craft and a small number of commercial fishing vessels.

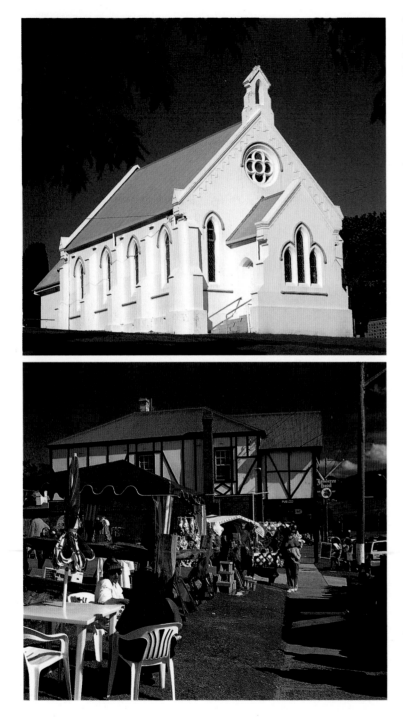

The Jamberoo Valley was settled by Europeans in the 1820s. After land was cleared, grazing began and within 10 years the village of Jamberoo had become a thriving, bustling community surrounded by fertile dairy farms. Landmarks around Jamberoo include seven pioneer cemeteries, Terragong House (a Georgian-style home built in 1858 by former Kiama mayor John Marks), the Jamberoo Hotel (today's structure includes sections of the original 1857 building), Jamberoo Public School (built from local sandstone and cedar in 1878) and four churches dating from the 1860s.

Thrillseekers also visit Jamberoo to enjoy one of the region's most popular tourist attractions, Jamberoo Recreation Park, where mountain tobogganing, water slides and power boat rides are among a variety of fun activities to choose from.

The coastal villages of Gerringong and Gerroa, just 10 to 15 minutes south of Kiama, are also home to many historic landmarks. Probably the best known of these is the Sir Charles Kingsford Smith Memorial and Lookout at Gerroa, commemorating the famous aviator's second crossing of the Tasman to New Zealand in January 1933. Kingsford Smith chose a long, smooth stretch of Gerroa's Seven Mile Beach to begin his epic flight aboard the *Southern Cross*.

Gerringong's historical landmarks include the original 1876 police station, built from stone with walls 60 centimetres thick, as well as homesteads and cottages dating from the 1840s and four churches dating from 1874. Gerringong's boat harbour, now a popular picnic area with boat ramp and rock pool, was the site of the original 1851 jetty, once an important shipping link to Sydney. Gerringong Golf Club's 18-hole, par 72 course is among the most picturesque courses in the region.

Surrounded by farmland and buttressed by ocean, mountains and national parkland, these idyllic villages are popular residential retreats and tourist havens.

Above left: This striking painted bluestone church was constructed at Gerringong in 1883 using stone quarried 100m from the site. Originally the Congregational Church, it is now the place of worship for members of the Gerringong Uniting Church.

Left: Originally built in 1857, the renovated Jamberoo Hotel still retains its country feel and is an appealing backdrop to the monthly village market.

Right: The Jamberoo Valley's lush green pastures remain a perfect place for dairying, 180 years after land was cleared and farmers began to settle here.

Overleaf: Mount Pleasant Lookout, south of Kiama, affords a breathtaking view over Werri Lagoon and the township of Gerringong.

M I N I N G   A N D   I N D U S T R Y

The Illawarra's coal-smudged ocean cliffs were first reported in Sydney Town in 1797 by the survivors of the shipwrecked *Sydney Cove*. Excited by the potential discovery, Governor Hunter despatched George Bass to investigate. Although Bass returned with news of an extensive coal seam in the seaside cliffs of the northern Illawarra, the inaccessibility of the region meant that another 40 years were to elapse before a government geologist was sent to investigate the region's coal reserves.

In the meantime, extensive stands of cedar had been discovered and timber became the region's first industry. This was followed by dairying, after Liverpool farmer Charles Throsby came to the district in 1815 in search of feed for his drought stricken cattle.

Once investigated, seaside coalcliffs were found to outcrop in mountainsides. After several failed attempts at mining these, James Shoobert's Mount Keira colliery began operation in 1849. Shoobert's success signalled the dawning of a new era, one that was destined to change the Illawarra forever. Illawarra's coal industry suddenly began to look like a veritable gold mine – black and bottomless. More than a century later in the 1940s the region's coal reserves were estimated at a mammoth 11,000 million tonnes and described as the highest grade coal in NSW.

Over 150 years, hundreds of men and boys have lost their lives in Illawarra mining disasters. In 1887 when pit conditions were primitive, the work was back-breaking and safety issues had barely been addressed, a cave-in at Bulli colliery claimed 81 lives. Fifteen years later on the last day of July in 1902, Australia's worst mining disaster occurred when a rock fall at the Mount Kembla colliery caused highly inflammable gases to ignite. The resulting explosion killed 95 men and could be heard eight kilometres away. Despite advances in health and safety regulations and procedures, coal mining remains a dangerous occupation.

From 1850 onwards, new pits began to mushroom wherever high-grade coal was found and by 1880, 10 mines were being worked around Wollongong and several mining villages had developed to the north. 'Black gold' had become the mainstay of the Illawarra economy, servicing Sydney and Wollongong's energy needs and spawning new industry.

As coal could only be transported by ship to Sydney or overseas, long jetties soon sprung up at headlands and beaches protected from strong southerly winds. As coal mining continued to grow, the problems posed by the lack of a natural deep-water harbour became increasingly obvious. The colony's government finally addressed the issue in 1861 when work began to upgrade Wollongong Harbour at Belmore Basin. By 1895 more than 250,000 tonnes of cargo was leaving Wollongong Harbour annually.

In 1888, the completion of the Illawarra-Sydney rail link signalled an escalation in the region's industrial development. This received a further boost at the turn of the century when construction began on an extensive port, better suited to deep-sea ships and capable of future expansion. Port Kembla was an ideal site, being both close to the coal pits and accessible by rail and road. By 1930 its two breakwaters enclosed a deep-water port of more than 130 hectares. Today Port Kembla is ranked among the four biggest ports on Australia's east coast.

At Kiama, basalt was being quarried as the old century closed. The Illawarra's 'blue gold' was used in local buildings from the mid-1800s and was first shipped to Sydney in 1870. Basalt mining began at Bass Point in Shellharbour 10 years later and continues to be mined today in Shellharbour and Kiama.

In 1908 the region's first copper refinery opened, followed by a metal manufacturing factory and a fertilizer production plant. Yet it was Charles Hoskins' purchase of 162 hectares of land west of Port Kembla that became the deciding factor in shaping Illawarra industry. Hoskins' iron and steel works, set up in 1928, began producing steel in 1931. That same year, Hoskins joined with two British firms to become Australian Iron and Steel, which in 1935 was sold to Broken Hill Proprietary Company Limited (BHP).

BHP immediately embarked on an ambitious program of expansion, which continued into the 1950s. Another 640 hectares of land was purchased and by 1939 there were five open hearth furnaces and a continuous billet mill producing steel slabs. Post-World War II the steelworks continued to boom and Port Kembla was ranked as Australia's largest industrial complex.

Left: Illawarra miners maintain a long tradition of coal mining in the region, dating back to 1849, when James Schoobert's Mt Keira Colliery commenced operation. Today's miners work eight to 13-hour shifts in pits 500m underground and up to 9kms inward to the coalface.

In 1946 the steelworks employed 3500 people. This figure had doubled by 1953 and doubled again by 1961 when 15,000 workers were on the payroll and another 2000 worked at BHP collieries. By 1980, BHP's entire Illawarra operations had 23,000 employees. To remain competitive on world markets however, BHP had to take on new cost-efficient technology and shed labour. Under the Steel Plan of the mid-1980s, BHP reduced its steel workforce and injected a massive $1 billion in capital expenditure into the 21st century. Apart from upgrading old equipment and commissioning new plant, such as the $406 million No. 6 blast furnace, BHP also committed itself to environmental improvement plans worth $150 million.

These days BHP employs about 21,000 people in NSW, of whom just over 12,000 live and work in the Illawarra. The scope of BHP's Illawarra operations is considerable, running the nine divisions of Slab and Plate Products, Welded Beam Plant, Sheet and Coil Products, Refactories, Collieries, Research, Transport, Engineering and Information Technology. Together they generate considerable wealth for the Illawarra community and Australia as a whole.

BHP is also involved in several joint projects of major importance to the Illawarra. The Port Kembla Coal Terminal handles 15-16 million tonnes of coal each year and is owned and operated by a consortium of six companies with regional coal mining interests, including BHP. Nearing completion is the $1 billion Esso-BHP Bass Strait oil rig project and soon to begin is a $400 million Bass Strait to Port Kembla natural gas line that will be used to generate power at Bomaderry and Port Kembla. Tubemakers, now wholly owned by BHP, produces pressure tested, steel fabricated line pipe for oil and gas pipelines. It also manufactures small diameter precision steel tubing, used by the furniture, fencing and automotive markets.

While BHP is the region's undisputed industry leader, there are many other players that help make the Illawarra an economically dynamic community.

Collieries not owned by BHP operate at South Bulli and

Left: An aerial view of the industrial heartland of Port Kembla, showing the Port Kembla Coal Terminal, the Port Kembla Grain Terminal and part of BHP's extensive steel-making operations.

Above right: Uncoiling of the transfer bar at BHP's Hot Strip Mill. After reheating slabs of steel from the slab caster to 1180° C, the slabs pass through a set of rollers at the Reversing Roughing Mill to reduce thickness prior to coiling. As the coil of steel in the Hot Coil Box unwinds, crop shears cut a staight edge to the coil prior to the steel entering the Finishing Mill, where it is rolled to the required final thickness.

Right: Engineers at the Hot Strip Mill use specialised monitoring equipment to check the 'warm work-roll profile' at the completion of a rolling campaign.

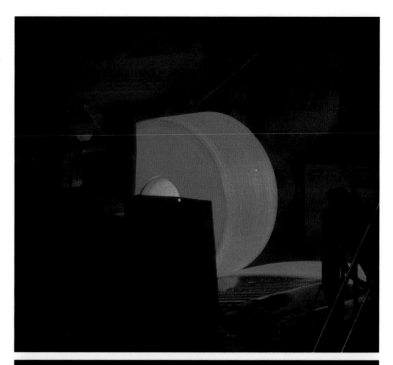

Helensburgh. The Corrimal and Illawarra Coke Works produce high-grade coking coal used at foundries and smelting plants across Australia and in South-East Asia. MMKembla Products manufactures copper tubing while Bisalloy Steel and Glastonbury Steel are involved in steel fabrication. Leussink Engineering, WGE and Wollongong Electrical Engineering provide engineering services to BHP and other companies elsewhere in Australia and overseas. BOC Gases' Port Kembla extraction plant produces nitrogen, oxygen and argon in liquid form that is used in BHP's steel-making processes. Plans are currently underway to reopen the Southern Copper plant at Port Kembla, which produced copper coil and extracted gold and silver in the manufacturing process. The Port Kembla Grain Terminal, located adjacent to the coal terminal at Port Kembla Harbour, handles grain from central and southern NSW to service export markets worth more than $1billion annually to Iran, Iraq, Egypt, Sri Lanka, Pakistan, China and the ever-increasing South-East Asian markets of Malaysia, Indonesia and Thailand.

In the region's south, Cleary Bros, Boral, Readymix, Pioneer and State Rail operate basalt quarries in Shellharbour and Kiama. Basalt, or blue metal, is used as road base and for road surfacing. It is also used as railway ballast and in the manufacture of concrete. The next wave of industry expected to make a major impact on the region are service industries such as telecommuting, specialising in design management, communication and computing.

Most of the Illawarra's industrial might is geographically located within Australia's Industry World, regarded as the most spectacular industrial complex in the southern hemisphere. The 700 hectare site features the BHP Visitors' Centre with its scale model of the steelworks; the BHP Steelworks Garden where 250,000 plants flourish; and self-guided tours of the Grain Terminal, Coal Terminal and Tom Thumb Lagoon.

Above left: The Port Kembla Grain Terminal is one of the most highly automated grain terminals in the world. Commissioned in 1989, the terminal has 30 storage bins with a total capacity of 260,000 tonnes and can achieve a vessel loading rate of 5000 tonnes per hour.

Left: Upon completion in late 1996 the 100,000 tonne, $400 million Esso oil platform will be the biggest and most complex rig ever installed in Bass Strait.

Right: The reclaimer unit at Port Kembla Coal Terminal transfers coal from the stockpile onto a conveyor system, which in turn transfers the coal onto vessels destined for Japan, India, Korea, China or Europe. During 1995 the terminal transferred 11.4 million tonnes of coal, earning an export income of more than US$450 million.

Overleaf: The dawn of a new day at Port Kembla's Inner Harbour.

MULTICULTURALISM

In the post-war economic boom of the 1950s the Illawarra began a change of face. Prior to this, the region's population had a distinct Anglo-Irish appearance. The Chinese market gardeners who'd arrived in the mid-1800s, although exotic, were few in number, and the region's indigenous owners could barely be counted 135 years after European settlement.

Today the Illawarra's population is made up of people from more than 80 countries worldwide. The move towards ethnic diversity began in the 1950s in response to massive expansion in the Australian steel industry. BHP exerted its might federally to gather support for mass immigration as a means to expand Australian manufacturing. During the 1950s, '60s and '70s, BHP maintained an itinerant, largely immigrant workforce drawn to the region by the promise of work and a good and rewarding life. A typical pattern set by migrants was to work at BHP for two or three years before moving on to better paid jobs or creating businesses that would turn homespun dreams of the lucky country into reality. For migrants, home-grown business was the best way out of unskilled factory work.

Prior to the 1950s, newcomers were mostly of Anglo-Irish background. During the post-war economic boom that followed immigrants began to arrive from elsewhere, led first by Germans and Dutch, followed by Italians and Greeks, then Eastern Europeans (often recruited from displaced people's camps) including Estonians, Lithuanians, Latvians, Ukranians and Poles. In the 1960s came Lebanese and Turks and more recently Macedonians. By 1980, more than 62 per cent of workers at Port

Left: The face of the Illawarra today – children from different cultures coming together to play and learn at Wollongong City Pre-School.

Above right: The Gypsy Flames Belly Dancers are well known throughout the Illawarra, performing at a variety of events throughout the year. Here, the popular troupe perform a Turkish Gypsy dance, Sulukule, before an enthusiastic crowd at Wollongong's annual Folklorika festival.

Right: The Dion family are an Illawarra institution. Arriving in Australia in the gold rush years of the 1840's, the Dions found their way to the Illawarra in the early years of this century. At first they owned a market garden at Fairy Meadow but in 1923 the five Dion brothers (Barney and Les senior are pictured here) commenced the bus run which, more than 50 years ago, was affectionately dubbed 'the slow boat to China'. These days, Les Dion junior (pictured) is on track to replace the family fleet with new buses by the turn of the century.

Kembla were born overseas and more than half were from a non-English speaking background. Vietnamese were among the last to arrive and the region's largest group of new arrivals are the 1500 overseas students, mostly Asian, who annually attend the University of Wollongong. Since the 1950s, chain migration has united migrants with family members.

While the post-war migrant boom meant a healthy boost to the region's steel industry, it also signalled a gradual shift for the region, particularly Wollongong, from a village way of life towards fostering of the arts and multiculturalism. Multiculturalism has added great depth to the fabric of life in the Illawarra – through dance, music, theatre, the visual arts, food, sport and religious worship.

The region's ethnic diversity is expressed through the large number of cultural associations; through sporting groups; through patronage of the arts at Wollongong City Gallery and artwork exhibited at small galleries across the region; through a tantalizing range of exotic cuisines; and through annual celebrations and religious events.

The region's restaurants and eateries offer dishes from all over the world, from French and German to Italian, Mexican, Chinese, Korean, Indian, Japanese, Thai and Vietnamese.

Wollongong enjoys various cultural spectacles, including the annual Folklorika, the Illawarra's largest ethnic festival. Held mid-year, Folklorika presents a colourful parade of people from differing ethnic backgrounds, food and crafts, music and dance.

The Illawarra boasts more than 30 choirs of non-English speaking background and community language schools operate across the region, teaching children the language of their parents' birth.

Today, the Illawarra is now the most ethnically diverse region in Australia. It's also a homogenous community, with no history of racial violence. Instead it nurtures understanding between peoples from all over the world.

Above left: The game of chess attains larger than life proportions on a daily basis in Wollongong Mall, when players from Greek, Italian and Macedonian communities try out their skills amidst the company of friends and onlookers.

Left: The Illawarra is now home to people from more than 80 different countries, who enjoy celebrating the cultural traditions of their place of birth. Here, women from the Australian Philippine Association perform a Muslim courtship dance from the island of Mindanao at the Folklorika festival.

Right: Flaminio Fina left his native Italy in 1960 to seek a new life in Australia and his sister Filomina (centre) followed in 1967. While working at the steelworks and later in his delicatessen, Flaminio dreamed of making pasta and in 1986 he opened 'Pasta Fina' in Crown Street. Tina De Francesco (right) was employed when they first opened and remains an enthusiastic worker in the business ten years later.

NAN TIEN

Rising majestically from Flagstaff Hill, adjacent to the F6 Freeway at Berkeley, Nan Tien is the largest Buddhist temple in the southern hemisphere. The temple is Australian headquarters of the Taiwanese-based Fo Kuang Shan sect, which has hundreds of millions of followers worldwide and more than 30,000 followers in Australia.

Following lobbying from local Buddhists and encouragement from Wollongong City Council, Fo Kuang Shan's Grand Master decided in 1990 that Wollongong, with its close proximity to Sydney, was an ideal site for the temple. After years of planning and construction, the lavish $50 million Chinese-style temple opened amid great fanfare in October 1995. Melding East and West in design and finish, Nan Tien's startling saffron, terracotta and fuchsia colour scheme is traditional to Fo Kuang Shan.

The main temple of the 22-hectare site is strategically positioned at equal angles between the mountain peaks of Mount Kembla and Mount Keira. Its magnificent roof structure, enclosed with more than 180,000 terracotta tiles, sweeps in curves from the eaves to the ridges, which are capped by dragons, seahorses, lions and deities. Surrounded by meticulously manicured gardens, complete with reflection ponds, the temple area is adorned with thousands of gold statues of Buddha.

Designed to become part of the wider Illawarra community, the temple complex has many halls, a library, a museum, dining rooms, dormitories and a state-of-the-art conference auditorium. Its multi-functional design allows it to serve both as a place of worship and an educational and cultural centre. It is predicted that once the temple is fully operational it will attract more than 200,000 visitors each year, making it an important tourist attraction for the region.

While a path is open at Nan Tien for those who are interested in studying the teachings of Buddha, monks and nuns at the temple say their main wish is for Buddha's teachings to improve the everyday lives of Illawarra people and all Australians.

Left: Literally meaning 'paradise of the southern hemisphere', Nan Tien is Australian headquarters of the Fo Kuang Shan Buddhist sect.

Above right: The tapering eight-storey pagoda overlooking the temple grounds has been erected to accommodate the cremated remains of departed worshippers.

Right: Monks at Nan Tien are devoted to 'humanitarian' Buddhism, enacted through cultural activities as well as educational, medical, social and charitable programs.

UNIVERSITY OF WOLLONGONG

There was once a time when Illawarra students travelled to Sydney to further their education. To become a lawyer or attain a trade or technical qualification it was necessary to leave the region, which lacked tertiary facilities.

The pathway to academia began to widen in 1928 when the region's first trades school and technical college opened in North Wollongong to service the needs of the region's growing industrial base. By the early 1950s, the Wollongong Trades School and Technical College had shifted further towards academia, firstly as a division of the NSW University of Technology then 10 years later as a college of the University of NSW. With an eye to the future, in 1953 about 100 hectares of prime land was purchased alongside the college at the foot of Mt Keira, adjacent to Wollongong Botanic Garden and just three kilometres from the city centre.

In the early 1960s, a campaign began for the flourishing tertiary college to attain university status of its own. The stepping stone towards this goal was the opening in March 1962 of Wollongong University College as a campus of the University of NSW. With 280 students and 24 teachers, the college offered science and engineering courses geared towards the needs of the region's ever-growing heavy industry. Within four years the college had expanded its course core to include language, general studies and commerce.

When the University of Wollongong was finally established in 1975 it became Australia's 18th university, offering degree courses in the faculties of engineering, humanities, mathematics, science and social sciences. Within two years the university had more than 2500 students and 150 academic staff.

During the 1980s the university underwent a period of enormous growth and development, unmatched in Australian university history, which was dubbed 'the McKinnon era'. Vice Chancellor Ken McKinnon's 13-year tenure with the university, which ended with his retirement in 1994, yielded an unprecedented 15 new buildings, including the Hope Theatre, the aptly named McKinnon

Left: With its proximity to both the centre of Wollongong and Pacific Ocean, Wollongong University is unique among Australian tertiary institutions. The beauty of its environs, combined with an outstanding academic record, make it the most popular university nationally for students from overseas and is also a major drawcard for the university's 10,500 Australian students.

Building and the Communication Centre. Expansive landscaping created the idyllic greenfield environment that characterises the university today.

By 1991, the university had added informatics, law, journalism and nursing to its courses. The following year the university moved off-shore for the first time when it agreed to provide post-graduate degree courses to the staff of Indonesian steel company Krakatoa. This was followed in 1993 by its establishment of an Institute of Australian Studies at Dubai in the United Arab Emirates. There, English language students can enrol in degree courses in business, the arts and computing. Also in 1993, in a move that realised the potential of open learning, the university launched an agreement with SBS Television to broadcast postgraduate courses.

Since the late 1980s the university has established several satellite campuses. Modelled on Canberra's Questacon, the hands-on Science Centre at campus east in Fairy Meadow is open to the public and has more than 120 interactive exhibits as well as a breathtaking planetarium. The Wollongong Conservatorium of Music at Gleniffer Brae in Keiraville caters to pre-tertiary music education while the Graham Park Campus 10 kilometres north of Nowra was established to better serve students from the Shoalhaven and Southern Highlands.

In 1994, a Federal Government review placed Wollongong among the top nine universities nationally. It was the only regional university to attain such status. This outstanding progress was reinforced by its top-group ranking in the Federal Government's 1995 Quality Review.

From humble beginnings as a trade school, Wollongong University has evolved into a cosmopolitan campus with students from all over Australia and more than 70 countries worldwide. Today, the university's nine faculties of creative arts, commerce, arts, education, engineering, informatics, health and behavioural sciences, law and science, attract 12,000 enrolments annually, including 1500 from overseas, and it is recognised as an important contributor to the economy of the Illawarra.

Above left: As part of their course in ecology and evolution, science students observe fruit fly in one of the university's well equipped, modern laboratories.

Left: Overlooked by mighty Mt Keira, Wollongong University's Olympic pool is part of the Recreation and Sports Association.

Right: The beautiful historic buildings of 'Gleniffer Brae' now accommodate the Wollongong Conservatorium of Music, a satellite campus of Wollongong University that teaches music literacy to the region's pre-tertiary students.

THE ARTS

The Illawarra's lush rainforests, sweeping coastline and pastoral plains first captured the imagination of visiting artists early in the 1800s. Probably the most important of these artists was Viennese born Eugene von Guérard, a former court painter to the King of Austria, who painted several views of the Illawarra after a two week visit to the region in the 1850s. English-born artist Conrad Martens' *Lake Illawarra* painted in 1835 presented tropical vegetation and shorelines cradling distant views of the escarpment, while *View of the Five Islands* (1861) captured the famous view from the escarpment edge. Landscape works by high-calibre colonial artists such as von Guérard, Martens, John Skinner Prout and George Angas contributed greatly to the Illawarra's reputation as the Garden of New South Wales. Works by these artists and many others can be viewed at Wollongong City Gallery, which boasts an outstanding collection of colonial art as well as a fine collection of Aboriginal art that focuses on West Arnhem Land and the Central Desert.

Although visiting artists were the first to express their impressions of the Illawarra, it wasn't until the 1950s that the first Art Society was formed, followed by the Wollongong Ceramic Society. The region's post-World War II influx of migrants further boosted the arts by introducing the artistic and cultural heritages of more than 80 countries worldwide to the Illawarra. It was Welsh miners who brought music and singing to the region whilst northern Britons contributed their love for band music. Choral work flourished and by the 1890s Wollongong was holding its own eisteddfod, which today continues as one of the oldest and largest in NSW.

The Illawarra has produced many outstanding performers and musicians, including Phantom of the Opera stars Anthony Warlow and Danielle Everett, pianists Marilyn Meier and Ambre Lyn Hammond, composers Barry Cunningham and Andrew Schultz, Australian Chamber Orchestra leader Richard Tognetti, Brussels

Left: Von Guérard's 'View of Lake Illawarra with distant mountains of Kiama' was worked from pencil sketches and studies produced during a two-week visit to the region late in the 1850s. Thanks to a private bequest, the painting was purchased by the Wollongong City Gallery from the Alan Bond collection in 1992 for $352,000.

Right: Bert Flugelman's 'Flight' sculpture is an outstanding tribute to Illawarra aviation pioneer Lawrence Hargrave. The 6330kg stainless steel 'silver bird', commissioned by the Friends of Wollongong University, was airlifted to its escarpment resting place at Mt Keira in 1989.

Opera House conductor Mirion Powell and contemporary jazz singer Vince Jones. The Conservatorium of Music, based at Gleniffer Brae Manor House, fosters the musical talents of the region's young people. Set in magnificent grounds at the foot of the escarpment at Keiraville, the conservatorium's youth and junior choirs, its BHP Youth Orchestra and numerous ensembles perform regularly at Gleniffer Brae and in Wollongong.

The Illawarra nurtures a vibrant theatrical environment, led by Theatre South, a dynamic and innovative company that stages co-operative shows with the university and fosters the talent of new playwrights, including the now nationally acclaimed writer of *Windy Gully*, Mount Kembla resident Wendy Richardson. The Illawarra also boasts several amateur theatre companies, including The Arcadians, Roo Theatre, Powerhouse Theatre Company, Stanwell Park Amateur Theatre, Wollongong Workshop Theatre and Guild Theatre. Since opening in Wollongong's CBD in 1988, the Illawarra Performing Arts Centre has been a popular venue for live theatre and musical performance as well as an important focal point for community and cultural events.

The Illawarra's literary talents include Kiama-born writer and columnist Charmian Clift, who married Australian writer George Johnston; women's activist/writer Dale Spender who once taught at Dapto High School; and poet/university lecturer Ron Pretty who co-founded Five Islands Press. Escarpment hide-aways in Wollongong's northern suburbs are the favoured abodes of several well-known writers, including Peter Corris, Jean Bedford and Robert Hood. Probably the region's greatest claim to literary excellence, however, was a visit by English author D H Lawrence, whose book, *Kangaroo*, was written from Wywurk, a bungalow overlooking the Pacific Ocean at Thirroul.

Earlier still, it's thought that Robert Louis Stevenson, author of *Treasure Island* and *Kidnapped*, also visited the region during the 1890s. A treacherous train journey through the slip-prone northern mining villages is believed to have inspired Stevenson to devote a chapter to storms, trains and mountain mud slides in his little known book, *The Wrecker*.

Above left: From their home in Wollongong's far northern suburbs, best selling authors Peter Corris and Jean Bedford write across a spectrum of genres, including crime, romance, biography and sport.

Left: The vocal talents of the region's young people are fosterd by the Conservatorium of Music's Junior Choir, pictured here performing at a concert during Senior Citizens' Week.

Right: Formed in 1986, the BHP Youth Orchestra, whose members range in age from mid-teens to early 20s, performs four major concerts each year.

SPORT AND LEISURE

Pass by an Illawarra sports field any day or night and you can guarantee there'll be a sporting team or two engaged in serious play. If there is a game to be played or a sporting endeavour to be pursued, it's certain to be happening in the Illawarra. Put a bunch of locals together, then toss them a ball, and before you know it a trophy has been named and the play-offs have begun.

The fact is, Illawarra people are sport crazy. They always have been. Participation in sport is high and support for athletes, players and clubs is keen. The Illawarra is a fiercely competitive region. Sport lovers possess an almost ferocious appetite for victory, be they armchair enthusiast, amateur or professional. The community champions top athletes, and over the years a select few have been elevated to star status.

Probably the Illawarra's most loved and best recognised international sporting figure is motorcycle hero Wayne Gardner, winner of the 1987 500cc World Motorcycle Championship. Born and bred in Balgownie, Gardner's first motorcycle was a wreck bought for $5 from a rubbish tip. From these humble beginnings Gardner cemented his place in Australian sporting folklore by winning the first two Australian Motorcycle Grand Prix's at Phillip Island in 1989 and 1990.

The region's favourite sporting team is undoubtedly the Illawarra Steelers, who were finally accepted into the premiership league competition, the Winfield Cup in 1982. The Steelers' first test representative was Rod Wishart, who wore the green and gold jersey for the first time in 1991, followed by Paul McGregor, who played his first test in 1994. These players follow in the footsteps of legends such as Tommy Kirk, Mick Cronin, Noel Mulligan, Keith Barnes, Bob Fulton and current coach Allan McMahon.

The region's, and the nation's, oldest sporting hero is 1932 Los Angeles Olympic Games gold medalist Edgar 'Dunc' Gray. Born in 1906, Dunc, a Kiama resident, rode to victory in cycling's 1000m time trial. More than 60 years later, Wollongong cyclist Joshua Kersten rose

Left: The Illawarra Steelers kick off in a home game at the Steelers Stadium during the 1996 competition. The Steelers entered the premiership competition in 1982 when it was called the Winfield Cup, reaching the finals for the first time in 1992.

Above right: Australia's oldest Olympian is 90 year old cyclist 'Dunc' Gray from Kiama, who rode to gold in the 1932 Los Angeles Olympics 1000m time trial.

Right: Three times Australian javelin champion Louise McPaul represented Australia at the '96 Atlanta Olympics and already has her sights set firmly on Sydney 2000.

to international prominence and carved a place for himself in future Olympic stakes when he won the 1996 world junior cycling championship.

The Illawarra has also produced Olympic gold medalist swimmer Beverly Whitfied as well as champion ironmen Darren and Dean Mercer, Jonathon Crowe and Phil Clayton, Australian duathalon champion Jonathon Hall, 1995 world superbike competition runner-up Troy Corser, world sailboard champion Natasha Sturges and surfing great and former Australian champion Terry Richardson as well as current fifth world champion Todd Prestage.

Illawarra athletes who competed at the 1996 Atlanta Olympic Games were marathon runner Kerryn McCann, javelin throwers Louise McPaul and Andrew Currey, 400 metres runner Kylie Hanigan, kayakers Brian Morton, Matthew Pallister and Andrew Wilson, sailboarder Natasha Sturges, baseballer Stuart Thompson and gymnast Kirsty-Leigh Brown.

The Illawarra's obsession with sport belies a spirit and determination that stems from the region's labouring roots. Sport was the main leisure activity, enjoyed at little expense by everyone, young and old. Today, sport remains a major vehicle for social activity across the region.

The Illawarra's temperate environment is ideal for sport lovers and outdoor sport is a year-round event. The flat lowlands buttressing the ocean north to south are rich in parks and ovals, where generations of locals have learnt to play their favourite sport. There can be no better place to kick a ball than oceanside at Bulli, Woonona, Towradgi or East Corrimal. Cyclists, rollerbladers and joggers make use of the most scenically beautiful cycleway in the nation, stretching as it does for 40 kilometres from Thirroul in the north to Shellharbour in the south. Where better to play a round of golf than at Gerringong, where stories abound about 'that hole in one' straight into the ocean. Cricket balls, and even footballs, also get lost in the surf after emission from Kiama's seaside sports field.

Many of the region's sporting stars have been nurtured at the Illawarra Academy of Sport, reputed as the best regional sporting

Above left: Illawarra Hawks basketballers Marc Brandon (left), Terry Johnson (centre) and Jason Bretell were born and bred in the Illawarra.
Left: The 18 foot skiffs, fastest and most exciting of the sailing classes, have one race each season on Lake Illawarra.
Right: The Illawarra coastline's rock platforms offer some of the best rock fishing in Australia. Experienced anglers say the month of May is the the best time to make their catch, when schools of tailor and salmon are making their annual northward migration. Throughout the year though, catches of snapper, bream, drummer and luderick are not uncommon.

facility for young Australians in the country. The Fairy Meadow based academy opened in the mid-1980s to develop the potential of talented young sportspeople from Wollongong, Shellharbour, Kiama, Wingecarribee and Shoalhaven. The academy has 185 students, aged 12 to 19, who hold scholarships in their chosen fields of rugby league, rugby union, soccer, cricket, netball, basketball, hockey or cycling. The academy has produced sporting stars such as one-day cricketer Shane Lee, world junior cycling champion Joshua Kersten and Illawarra Steelers rugby league captain John Cross.

The region has grown rich in international class sporting facilities, led firstly by the Steelers Stadium, situated seaside at Wollongong. A $24 million stadium upgrade currently underway will increase spectator capacity to 20,000. Beaton Park Athletics Centre is a world class track, earmarked for use by local and international athletes during the lead-up to the Sydney 2000 Olympic Games. Wollongong University has a first class Olympic pool and hockey fields and the Illawarra is dotted with dozens of beautifully manicured bowls lawns.

Soccer fans flock to Brandon Park, home to the Wollongong Wolves. For more than 20 years the Wolves have played in national competition, producing past champion Bob Young and current stars Robert Middleby and captain Matt Horsley.

The Illawarra Hawks basketball team might be one of the smallest clubs in the National Basketball League, but it has a huge local following and has repeatedly reached the play-offs. The only association-administered basketball club in the league (the rest are commercially or privately owned), the Hawks most famous player to date has been former Olympic team guard Gordon McLeod, who now coaches at the Institute of Sport in Canberra.

A fairly recent addition to the region's sporting arena is the Illawarra Flame Baseball Club, which finished second in its debut season with the NSW-Sydney major league in 94-95 and which aims to enter national competition by the Year 2000. Baseball has become the fastest growing junior sport in the region, rivalled only by netball, which has about 7000 junior and senior players who compete year round, indoor and outdoor, day and night, week days and weekends. Growth sports include touch footy, played day and night by about 5000 people across the region.

Right: Lake Illawarra is a focus for water-based recreational activities in the region, including, fishing, sailing, sailboarding and waterskiing.

P H O T O G R A P H I C   I N F O R M A T I O N

The photographs in this book were taken using Art Panorama, Mamiya RZ67, Linhof Master Technika 5x4 and Canon EOS 1 cameras, utilising a range of lenses. Filters were used occasionally to improve the quality of the images: a polarising filter controlled reflected light thereby improving colour saturation, a graduated filter was used when required to control overexposure of the sky and an 81C filter was used in heavy shade for added warmth.

All photographs were taken on Fuji professional transparency film. The outstanding sharpness and beautiful colour rendition exhibited by the family of Fuji films made them our films of choice.

ALSO BY THE SAME AUTHORS......

AUSTRALIA BENEATH THE SOUTHERN CROSS

Sue and Brian Kendrick travelled Australia for 18 months to collect the stunning photographs for their best-selling book **Australia Beneath the Southern Cross**. From the temperate rainforests of Tasmania to the deserts of central Australia and the rugged gorges of the Kimberley they jouneyed more than 55,000 kilometres and shot in excess of 7,000 photographs. Avoiding cities and towns they travelled to some of the most remote and isolated regions of the continent, into the **real** outback.

Take advantage of the special reader's price of $30.00 and join the thousands who have already experienced the splendour of this ancient continent, celebrated in **Australia Beneath the Southern Cross.** 180 pages full colour, hard back

THE SHOALHAVEN
South Coast New South Wales

The first in a series of books on regional Australia, **The Shoalhaven** depicts the history, natural beauty and industries of this beautiful section of the New South Wales south coast. Wander the historic towns of Milton and Berry, take a look inside the studio of artist Arthur Boyd and discover the region's many parks and reserves. Look at the area's active farming and manufacturing industries and visit HMAS Creswell and HMAS Albatross. Enjoy the atmosphere, the people and the places of the Shoalhaven. Price $19.95, 72 pages full colour, hard back.

FRAMED PRINT COLLECTION.......

Selected images from Sue and Brian's books **The Illawarra** and **The Shoalhaven** are now available as framed prints. Reproduced on 128 GSM gloss art paper, this wonderful collection will make a stunning addition to home or office. All prints are framed using black aluminium moulding with colour co-ordinated matts and are ready to hang. Other prints are also available from the Lightstorm collection. For information please phone (044) 466 007. Please note that prints are **not** available unframed.

NB: To place your order please use a photocopy of the order form on the opposite page.

FRAMED PRINT COLLECTION

01

02

03

04

05

06

Post to: Lightstorm Photography Pty Ltd. P.O.Box 1167 Nowra NSW 2541
Australia Phone orders: (044) 466 007 Fax orders: (044) 466 008

QTY	DESCRIPTION		ITEM	PRICE	TOTAL
	SEVEN MILE BEACH	590mm x 315mm	01	39.95	
	WOLLONGONG HARBOUR	590mm x 315mm	02	39.95	
	FISHING BOAT	590mm x 315mm	03	39.95	
	CORAL TREE SILHOUETTE	590mm x 315mm	04	39.95	
	PIGEON HOUSE MOUNTAIN	340mm x 310mm	05	34.95	
	MINNAMURRA FALLS	310mm x 340mm	06	34.95	
	AUSTRALIA BENEATH THE SOUTHERN CROSS		Book	30.00	
	THE SHOALHAVEN		Book	19.95	
	ADD FREIGHT : AUSTRALIA $7.50				

I enclose my cheque/money order made payable to
Lightstorm Photography Pty Ltd   **TOTAL $**
or debit my   ☐ VISA   ☐ MASTERCARD ☐ BANKCARD ☐ AMEX

CARD No. ☐☐☐☐ ☐☐☐☐ ☐☐☐☐ ☐☐☐☐   Expiry date___/___

Name _____

Address_____

_____ Postcode _____ Phone ( ) _____

Signature _____

First published 1996
© Copyright photographs Sue and Brian Kendrick 1996
© Copyright text Gillian Cumming 1996
Designed by Brian Kendrick
Printed by Dai Nippon

National Library of Australia Cataloguing-in-Publication data
Kendrick, Sue.
The Illawarra: between the mountains and the sea.

ISBN 0 9586745 0 7.

1. Illawarra (N.S.W.) – Pictorial works.
2. Illawarra (N.S.W.) – Description and travel.
3. Illawarra (N.S.W.) – History.
I. Kendrick, Brian.
II. Cumming, Gillian.
III. Title.
994.46

Many thanks to:
John Craigie for producing the map on page 7
Wollongong Aerial Patrol for assistance with the aerial photographs

Our sincere appreciation to the following individuals and organisations who have helped with this publication:
BHP Collieries Division; BHP Steel Division; Jean Bedford; Peter Corris; The Councils of Wollongong, Shellharbour and Kiama;
Dions Buses; Edgar 'Dunc' Gray; The Illawarra Hawks; The Illawarra Mercury; The Kersten brothers; Kiama Visitors' Centre;
Minnamurra Rainforest Visitors' Centre; Nan Tien Temple; North Wollongong Life-savers; Panorama Hotel Restaurant; Pasta Fina;
Louise McPaul; The Port Kembla Coal Terminal; The Port Kembla Grain Terminal; The Rhododendron Park; The Steelers;
The University of Wollongong; Wollongong Aerial Patrol; Wollongong City Gallery; Wollongong City Pre-School;
Wollongong Conservatorium of Music; Wollongong Reference Library.

Sue and Brian would like to thank their friends the Mustos
and Gillian would like to thank her family